INSIDE OF ME

IF I FEEL...

Mimes: Steve Budas
          Kym Longhi

Actors: John Bentley
          Eva Two Crow
          Jeanne Young

Written and Photographed
by Nancy Lee Walter

Inside of Me If I Feel...

Copyright © 1993 Nancy Lee Walter

Without limiting the rights under copyright reserved above, no part of this publication may be reproduced, stored in or introduced into a retrieval system, or transmitted, in any form or by any means (electronic, mechanical, photocopying, recording or otherwise), without the prior written permission of the above copyright owner/publisher of this book.

Write to: Naturally by Nan
P.O. Box 132
Rosemount, MN 55068

ISBN 0-9635127-3-0

MANUFACTURED IN THE UNITED STATES OF AMERICA
Printer: Bolger, St. Paul, Minnesota

PRINTED ON RECYCLED PAPER

To Matthew Thomas Walter
whose life and death
marked a path
for spiritual growth in others.

ACKNOWLEDGMENTS

This book has been the collective effort of several wonderful people. They have given of their talents and expertise generously.

We are appreciative of Rev. Theodore P. Kalkwarf, M.Div., M.A., Louise Griffith, M.A., L.P. and Richard R. Rudie, Licensed Consulting Psychologist for their technical assistance in the field of therapy and counseling.

In addition our appreciation is extended to: Irene Conroy and Marion Dane Bauer as literary consultants, Kirsten Ford as book design consultant, Gail Steel as publishing consultant, Eric O. Haugen, Esq. and Vicki M. Ahl, Esq. for legal assistance, Jay Jaffey, Steve Loff, Molly Faulk and Anna Smith for applied therapeutic critiquing, Katy Skobba and her First Grade Students at Hidden Valley Elementary, Burnsville, Minnesota for field testing this text, the Madras, Oregon Senior High School "Be Yourself II" class for innovative script input, Yvonne C. Olson and H. Bruce Smith of Pillsbury House for photo session scheduling, Pillsbury House Community Center for photo session work space, Gemma Irish, Ute Outlaw, Jeremy Westenberg, Adam Westenberg, Andrew Westenberg and Shashi Olivier for donated props, Gail Irish and Kenneth L. Walter for moral support, Fran Eno, Nadeane Silbernagel, Marilyn Ayres-Broaddus and Rude Valle, Lois Moffit and Carol Bromer for creative marketing input, Janelle Walter for typesetting and design, Katrina Walter-Eggers for typeset consultation, Scott Bouman, Russell Nelson, Michael Mazer, Jorge Triana, Olson Graphic Products, Inc. and Pierce Art Center (Bob Day owner) for photographic consultation and support and John Iverson, Jason Haugen, Su Quarstad and Christopher Gross for photographic assistance.

Thank you for inviting us into your library. We hope to be a helpful friend to young people.

In this text you will find that it is important to remember that feelings just are. They are neither good nor bad. It is our choices of acting on them that count.

Nancy L Walker

When I cut my finger,

I put a bandage on it.

When
I feel
hurt
inside,

I don't know where to put the bandage.

If I feel cold,

I put
on a
coat.

But when I feel left out,

putting on
a coat
doesn't help.

I can't hear

or see
the feelings
inside
of me.

I can't fix my feelings.

But I can choose how to act on them.

If I feel angry

because a friend teases me,

I can choose to hit her,

hit a pillow

or tell her how I feel.

What would you do?

If I feel frustrated,

I can choose to talk to

someone I trust, slam doors

What would you do?

I can choose to...

or

What would you do?

I can choose to...

or

If I feel adventurous,

I can choose to...

or

If
I feel
jealous,

I can choose to...

or

If I feel silly,

I can choose to...

If I feel hopeful,

I can choose to...

If I feel worried,

I can choose to...

And if
I feel
gloomy,

I can choose to...

I'm a valuable person.

Too valuable to bury my feelings.

It's O.K. to tell people how I feel...

in a way that
doesn't hurt
them or me.

They may like it

or they may
not like it.

But I feel
better
being honest.